The National Poetry Series was established in 1978 to ensure the publication of five collections of poetry annually through five participating publishers. The Series is funded annually by Amazon Literary Partnership, the Gettinger Family Foundation, Bruce Gibney, HarperCollins Publishers, Stephen King, Lannan Foundation, Newman's Own Foundation, Anna and Olafur Olafsson, Penguin Random House, the Poetry Foundation, Elise and Steven Trulaske, and the National Poetry Series Board of Directors.

2018 COMPETITION WINNERS

Valuing
by Christopher Kondrich of University Park, MD
Chosen by Jericho Brown for University of Georgia Press

Nervous System
by Rosalie Moffett of Athens, GA
Chosen by Monica Youn for Ecco

Fear of Description
by Daniel Poppick of New York, NY
Chosen by Brenda Shaughnessy for Penguin Books

It's Not Magic
by Jon Sands of New York, NY
Chosen by Richard Blanco for Beacon Press

Eyes Bottle Dark with a Mouthful of Flowers
by Jake Skeets of Vanderwagen, NM
Chosen by Kathy Fagan for Milkweed Editions

EYES BOTTLE DARK *with a*

MOUTHFUL *of* FLOWERS

EYES BOTTLE DARK *with a* MOUTHFUL *of* FLOWERS

poems by

JAKE SKEETS

MILKWEED EDITIONS

Published 2019 by Milkweed Editions
Printed in Canada
Cover design by Mary Austin Speaker
Cover photograph by Richard Avedon,
© The Richard Avedon Foundation
19 20 21 22 23   5 4 3 2 1
First Edition

Milkweed Editions, an independent nonprofit publisher, gratefully acknowledges sustaining support from the Ballard Spahr Foundation; the Jerome Foundation; the McKnight Foundation; the National Endowment for the Arts; the Target Foundation; and other generous contributions from foundations, corporations, and individuals. Also, this activity is made possible by the voters of Minnesota through a Minnesota State Arts Board Operating Support grant, thanks to a legislative appropriation from the arts and cultural heritage fund. For a full listing of Milkweed Editions supporters, please visit milkweed.org.

Library of Congress Cataloging-in-Publication Data

Names: Skeets, Jake, author.
Title: Eyes bottle dark with a mouthful of flowers : poems / Jake Skeets.
Description: First edition. | Minneapolis, Minnesota : Milkweed Editions, 2019.
Identifiers: LCCN 2019001875 (print) | LCCN 2019003038 (ebook) |
   ISBN 9781571319920 (ebook) | ISBN 9781571315205 (pbk. : alk. paper)
Subjects: LCSH: Navajo Indians--Poetry.
Classification: LCC PS3619.K46 (ebook) | LCC PS3619.K46 A6 2019 (print) |
   DDC 811/.6—dc23
LC record available at https://lccn.loc.gov/2019001875

Milkweed Editions is committed to ecological stewardship. We strive to align our book production practices with this principle, and to reduce the impact of our operations in the environment. We are a member of the Green Press Initiative, a nonprofit coalition of publishers, manufacturers, and authors working to protect the world's endangered forests and conserve natural resources. *Eyes Bottle Dark with a Mouthful of Flowers* was printed on acid-free 100% postconsumer-waste paper by Friesens Corporation.

For my family, the strongest people I know

CONTENTS

Koodóó Hózhǫ́ǫ Dooleeł

From here, there will be beauty again

EYES BOTTLE DARK *with a* MOUTHFUL *of* FLOWERS

Drunktown

Indian Eden. Open tooth. Bone bruise. This town split in two.
Clocks ring out as train horns, each hour hand drags into a screech—
iron, steel, iron. The minute hand runs its fingers

                                               through the outcrops.

Drunktown. Drunk is the punch. *Town* a gasp.
In between the letters are boots crushing tumbleweeds,

                            a tractor tire backing over a man's skull.

—

Men around here only touch when they fuck in a backseat
                    go for the foul with thirty seconds left
                        hug their sons after high school graduation
                open a keg
            stab my uncle forty-seven times behind a liquor store

—

A bar called Eddie's sits at the end of the world. By the tracks,
drunk men get some sleep. My father's uncle tries to get some
under a long-bed truck. The truck backs up to go home.

I arrange my father's boarding school soap bones on white space
and call it a poem. Like my father, I come upon death
staggering into the house with beer on the breath.

—

Mule deer splintered in barbed tendon. Gray highway
veins narrow—push, pull under teal and red hills.
A man is drunk-staggering into northbound lanes,
dollar bills for his index and ring fingers. Sands glitter
with broken bottles—greens, deep blues, clears, and golds.
This place is White Cone, Greasewood, Sanders,
White Water, Bread Springs, Crystal, Chinle, Nazlini,
Indian Wells, and all muddy roads lead from Gallup.
The sky places an arm on the near hills.
On the shoulder, dark gray—almost blue—bleeds

into greens

                                        blue-greens

turquoise into hazy blue

                              pure blue

no gray or gold

                        or oil black seeped through.

        —

If I stare long enough, I see my uncle in a mirror. The bottle caps we use for eyes.

—

An owl has a skeleton of three letters
o twists into *l*

the burrowing owl burrows
under dead cactus

feathers fall on horseweed
and skull bone blown open

Afterparty

We tank down beer. Eyelids lower and lower. He lets me
feel beneath his basketball shorts,

                                  sorrel fields along his thigh.
Burrows in our bellies heavy and heavy from rolling rock
and blue ribbon. Aluminum ghost coaxes his kiss. Candle
left lit. He mouths the neck and lip of another

                                  bottle—rifle
cold. My tongue coils on the trigger before its click.
Corn beetles scatter out

                                 no longer his bones.

– –

In the Fields

dogs
maul
remains
like white
space
does

Truck Effigy

purple paint fades into overcast sky

broken

     clouds   sanded down

               to metal teeth

carburetor muscle beneath combustion

clouds

     broken

         pockets of smoke

          blackening scalp

he swallows transmission and gasket

                              bonnet with full wings

torn from his burning back

an eye alters into alternator

            the other a hubcap

he becomes man returned to smolder

truck frame lodged into the graded roof

                  of his palate

locked with him at the wrists   his palms grip sunburnt skin

    he carousels a young boy   rocks propel into the air

       again again again again   he lets the steering wheel go he lets the boy go   body spun into the seat

    gravel-torn skin   his truck carousels

        hair threads into branches   over and over and over and over and his body not flown to the brushes

his body sown into the seat

and the truck and char and everything else

Tácheeh

boys swim in lake water
                          coming thunder
          they hold the other
try to hear a heartbeat
                    splash apart
hands petal on the shore
                          a spine
their bodies lap and tenor
                    they press their lips together
their torch skin
                          a distant sunset
                    distant headlight
          distant city
distant brushfire

—

they burrow roads for hot wheels
     discover entire towns

in damp soil
     roll tiny cars
back and forth to even roadways
     pack dirt with feet

shine die-cast metals with their shirts

     goose bumps
dot lower backs
       fingers
     wander beneath jeans

damp air curves
in around the navel

     they discover their names
as bottle caps beneath them
     the letters teethed

—

just boys still
veined hands latched to their necks

each eye a coal pearl
   for grandfathers returned to water

mothers held in their hair
   cousins at teeth

one carries his name
   like a cold sore

on their knees on vinyl tile
mistaken for water

on the kitchen floor
   after painting an ode

to sky bit down
on scar tissue in inner cheek

just another war
   wars in arm hair
in the tomatoes

   instead of a burning
their names become a cornfield

—

fingers lupine
        beardtongue
bee plant in harrow grasses

pronghorn in wild rose
        truck radio more sego lily
and pigweed spewing

        from open mouth
boys watch ricegrass shimmer in smoke

fires everywhere around them
        arms stretch in sap and bark
hair now meadow

limbs tangle into snakeweed
burning burning burning burning

they know becoming a man
means knowing how to become charcoal

staccato of ash
holding a match to their skin

trying not to light themselves on fire

Let There Be Coal

I.

A father hands a sledgehammer to two boys outside Window Rock.
The older goes first, rams a rail spike into the core, it sparks—

> no light comes, just dust cloud,
> > glitterblack.

The boys load the coal. Inside them, a generator station opens its eye.
A father sips coal slurry from a Styrofoam cup, careful not to burn.

II.

train
tracks
and
mines
split
Gallup
in two

Men
spit
coal
tracks rise
like a spine
when Drunktown
kneels to the east

III.

Spider Woman cries her stories coiled in warp and wool. The rug now hung
in a San Francisco or Swedish hotel.

We bring in the coal that dyes our hands black not like ash
but like the thing that makes a black sheep black.

IV.

This is a retelling of the creation story where Navajo people journeyed four worlds and God declared, "Let there be coal." Some Navajo people say there are actually five worlds.

Some say six.

A boy busting up coal in Window Rock asks his dad, "When do we leave for the next one?"
His dad sits his coffee down to hit the boy. "Coal doesn't bust itself."

Siphoning

his cousin trying to show him how to siphon
                         empty night greens
             with a growing storm
                             here comes the water

his palm white shell cupped around his ears
                               oceans and rains
                 returned in symphony on trachea
                                 of outcrop

find you a girl who can suck like this
                      wet rubber kisses
             boys are often the wind
                      always a howl

come on pussy come on fucking puss
                        he sucks and sucks
                 for the water
              but only tastes gasoline

Gasoline Ceremony

A woman breezes into a jail cell, her skirt hiked. The boy's eyes undress the man
first as his cousins' voices snap like twigs. The man's jumpsuit opens
first as the woman swallows him whole. The boy's groin flutters into a dragonfly
and drowns in the mucus on the floor.

Look at those tits.

This is the boy's first time watching porn. His mouth turned exhaust pipe.
Nerves spark
into bulb, almost lightning in the root.

I'm about to cum

His veins burst oil, elk black.

Virginity

Clouds in his throat,
six months' worth.

He bodies into me
half cosmos, half coyote.

We become night
on Bread Springs

road. Shirts off,
jeans halfway

down, parked
by an abandoned

trailer. "No one
lives here,"

he whispers.
We become porch

light curtained
by moth wings,

powdered into ash.

Maar

buffaloburr veins around siltstone
mounds on the monocline

flow rock smooths over into oar
cutleaf cornflower overgrown

pollen blown out
larkspur and beeplant on the meadow

grasp at the basement fault
taut atop diatreme

bulb liquid overflows into grasses
yellow sheen in the winds

laccolith ghost shadows over hungry dust
rains chew down medicine twigs

blue flax left as moans
that foam into the sky

numb star erect over the horizon
burning bomb quiet as stone

Swallowing Kept Secrets

Mornings turn out green thread. Alder
and safflower—wilds of this ilk—

bloom in bloodstream. His chin soaks in lactic acid,
chlorine, and zinc. Untwist from blankets

into aftersmoke. Hill sage cusp in his eye.

He mouths oxeye and antelope sage. Pinioned,
he removes his shirt again to unveil wood **rose**

and feather cindered black. He calls for the fires
as he undresses into nightjars.

Dust Storm

sandbur shiver in outflow
get at water coughed up

a snake contorts spackled
       dark puddle lilac
licked by heavy sun
       off smog soot

gust rack did up with cold front
he sees his body like a dead one

then as a mirror unbroken
thin as mosquito wing

clouds glutton rain
and tongues rope spun

best put as desire
       as marrow coiled in spine
as question marks unbuttoned
       so letters spill out

wasp eye corners
       heavy as wind
unfurl into him
       gulp on parch
knot into sediment

legs warp diamond twill among cactus
lightning leaks from lip

thunderhead
     craned down
the beak punctures
     pinacate beetle

virga carried
     on its back
he turns him
     on his back

before joints
     explode

into dust

       alkaline

fungi

    wild carrot root

        sown in strata

collect again

    on teeth

– –

DL N8V 4 3SOME

Cries through his hands echoed
      thunder palmed by sky.
Our dark limbs roll clouds

heavy over mid-May snow.
Stretch marks spider down to hip,

lightning bolts against the ice
on his sheets beneath us. Gasps
      for air between the cries

were his fists, punching holes
      in every wall.

Dear Brother

You kissed a man the way I do
                                   but with a handgun. You called it; I'm the fag
we were afraid to know, the one we'd throw rocks at, huff at like horses.

I learned to touch a man by touching myself. I learned to be a man by loving one.

Prison is not the chicken wire we'd get tangled in. Remember our bloodied
knees and bloody palms from mangled handlebars, beer bottles,
          and cactus spines? Remember the horned toad
                                   we didn't mean to kill?

Our silence—thick as the dust kicked up by our skinny legs. You are still
that silence. Still that boy holding a deflated body
                                   with your dawning hands.

Child Born of Water

I bend over, crescent spine. Bend again, reach back—
this is how I pleasure him, Father. Undo prayer, zipper.

Hands on neck, ankles.   Blister.
A god on knees.   God of slack.

Swallow God—come, downpour on canyon wall.
                We husk apart, machine pollen.

Father, I've been afraid of this lightning—
this man has me oceaned.

Thieving Ceremony

You've come for me twice before. Body swollen
with booze. Fires for eyes. Each time, I let you have me
                              and let you cry. Let me
                    heal you. It is your hands
that touch me. We become the black wool of a night sky
every time. Slide out of our clothes in a backseat,
                              in a back room,
                    black as a ye'ii mask.
We kiss, caesura to ensure the blackening. We are First Man
and Turquoise Boy ash-married in a ceremony that is ours now.
                    Make charcoal
              of the boys before us
who have only come to make love to the mass graves
in our teeth. To them our flesh is still soot, still furnace,
                         still jet, still a cornstalk
                    and juniper tree
                         left burning.

Buffalograss

Barely morning pink curtains
drape an open window. Roaches scatter,

the letter *t* vibrating in cottonwoods.
His hair horsetail and snakeweed.

I siphon doubt from his throat
for the buffalograss.

Seep willow antler press against
the memory of the first man I saw naked.

His tongue a mosquito whispering
its name, a hymn on mesquite,

my cheek. The things we see the other do
collapse words into yucca bone.

The Navajo word for *eye* hardens
into the word for *war.*

How to Become the Moon

He enters you, hide him, a silver dollar
                   beneath your pillow,

in a pawnshop, lodged in your throat. Your birthmark
will remind him of bruising, his father's belt, broom,

branch across his face. He will see his past in the whorl
                         of your hair

as you go down on him. He sees a boy, afraid of the deep end,
drowning in the swimming pool of your throat.
                      He swears your eyes are chlorine
            blue and black, you both purple soot.

He says *swallow* but do not,
            hold it as a secret

                     and kiss him
        so he can know you know him

               the way he can know him, a dark
moon rising from the pool water.
        The lights ribboned on his cheek
as he comes up for air.

Love Poem

You stand by your car, man in meadow
        now deep white—slow teeth, slow ice.

                Fallow-night footprints
            follow through stiff with each crunch in the snow.

        Frost crystals on my tongue.

Your cheekbone cold against my face,
    a whirring rock marrow deep.

—

I open the word and crawl inside its spine, barbed wire, turbine
with dark belly, coil hierarchy.

What word, you ask. Your body a cloud flattened in my hand.

Your body coiled with mine. Air snakes
over rib cage, cracks into powder.

I say *thorn*. I say *mouth*.

—

Desire is criminal. You being here is criminal.

You sip from the delta near my tongue. Ossuary
deepens at the clavicle.

Eyes stutter open. Limbs crepuscular over the bed frame.

I watch you shower after.
Tributaries, confluence, mineral stains.

You rub the holy off your skin. Your fingers
in after-soap jaw white.

—

Bent wasp hums behind your throat. In the iris,
orange whispers into deep yellow slather.

Uranium corrodes to spalling black,

speckles on hyoid horn. Your shoulder blades gawk open, wings sylphlike.
Torso woven with sweat chalks down to bone.

Skin can be too loud sometimes.

—

You have the night's bristle—yolk noose from penumbra.

I lick the railroad down your back—
                                admire black water in your hair.

                                Before you go,
I unbury the jaw. You swallow frozen sand.

I say *you can go now, you can go now.*

In the Fields

I palpate his chest, a tome, with skin like milk, bear-hued. Fingers hum across my forehead into a number. His eyes bloodshot and flaxen from the lamplight. My tongue runs across his shoulders, stone bells affixed to bone. Cathedral noise in the socket, a rotten lisp. Pipelines entrench behind his teeth. I hear a crack in his lung like burning coal. I hear his lips kissing mine as a sermon. My pelvis daises as he chants my body back to weeds. One day he'll forget about wounds and lower himself too into bellflower.

Naked

with lines from James Thomas Stevens

t'óó łichíí	naked or all red
hastįįh łichíí'go	man naked, man all red
łichíí'go	I am naked, I am all red
shida' łichíí'go	my uncle naked, my uncle all red
shínaaí łichíí'go	my brother naked, my brother all red

the closest men become is when they are covered in blood

or nothing at all

Comma

The comma is a heart murmur, tremor in hamstring. He is an *almost*; someone calling in time about the man staggering out of American Bar into traffic— mouths gasping into headlights.

He is headlights; two boys quickly push off each other. Commas dangling like belt buckles from their ankled jeans as they run out to the brushes.

More than pause—comma as toddler asleep on crisp sheets, body fetaled in big snow beneath I-40. Someone should call in time before the comma becomes a period,
his legs curled in against his body.

— —

Drift(er)

after Benson James, Drifter, Route 66, Gallup, New Mexico, 06/30/79
by Richard Avedon

Drift
to drift is to be carried by a current of air or water
                    but men are not the teeth
of their verbs
                                they pry nouns open with a belt buckle
                                            to take a sip

Drifter
a drifter carried by a current of air or water
                              makes his way from one place to another
                                    see *vagabond,* see *transient,* see *drunk*

see a man with shoulder-length hair
dollar bills fisted, standing before a white screen
see his lips how still
how horizon
how sunset

                                                            a train

passing through

I try to hug him

through the spine

left on the white space
        his face becomes a mirror
if I stare long enough
              my face
charcoaled
        pursed squinting
at the camera

train horn
        punch shatters
the mirror
            frees him from the page

my uncle leaps from the

In the Fields

                    c
              r
                 o
                    w
              s

           scavenge
           remains
             like

           l
                 e
                          t
                 t
                       e
              r
                 s

         on white space

The Body a Bottle

cracked hawkweed sacrum
nectar bitter from the flower

its pelvis dyed matter dark
petal to sepal frazzled

limp like a lazy eye
weed bud calcified

on a bottle of muddy gin
water swollen in the body

yellow madder crushed into sand
fresh blood oozes at the lips

the hair matted root
inlet of a river done in

Eyes Bottle Dark with a Mouthful of Flowers

metal sand and gravel chutes
halve a body half sun half shadow
a man but not   just an oil canister
choked on exhaust   a body but not

rail spike teeth tsk tsk tsked
as the kid heard the air horn
he listened to train tracks
say it would catch him if he would just only just only just only just only

jump

intestines blown into dropseed
strewn buffalograss blood clots
eyes bottle dark
mouth stuffed with cholla flower

barberry
yellow plant
greasebush
bitterweed

Glory

Native American male. Early twenties. About 6'2", 190 pounds.
Has the evening for a face.

—

Possible public intoxication. Native American female. No ID. She reported
being raped.
White shirt. No pants. Her legs swallowed the hotel.

—

Shots fired. Shots fired. Group of males scattered. Native American possibly.
One has a skull tattoo. Some ran east on Boardman. The skull is still here.

—

Medic unit requested. Sagebrush Bar.
Unidentified male not responsive. Possible hit-and-run.
Witnesses described it as a man being spit out from the mouth of a 4x4.

—

Yellow car heading north on Highway 666. Possible DWI. The car is kissing
the median like a wasp against a window.
Its wings torn to pieces.

—

I just saw a young boy get hit by a train. I don't know. I don't know. I don't
know. I don't know. He ran onto the tracks and the train hit him. It hit him.
He's still moving.   He's young. Maybe twenty. We're on the Westside
by Walmart. Should I help him? He's moving, he's moving.
The train hit him. There's blood all over him.
The train ate through him like a river eats through the arroyo. The train,
it sounds like a river.

> Like a river, a river goddamnit,
> a river, a river,

> ariverariverariverariverariverariverariver

a river

—

This is Officer Carson. Medic requested. Man down. Native male. Late twenties, early thirties. Stab wounds to the stomach. Pulse faint. Blood on the snow. He is being erased from the

Sleepers

When the going gets tough, launch reeds into the sky
                                    and escape on rainbows.

Maybe now, leave the body beneath tractor-trailers in the cutleaf

and look to the wounds in our bellies,

                    climb through.

—

*"The drunks picked up after the jail was crammed full used to sleep on the stairs
that led down from the old jail to the main of the Gallup City Hall. 'They used to
be called Sleepers.'"*
"Drunken Indians," New Yorker, *September 1971*

Sleepers in the fields with Mormon tea crowns. Bellflowers and sagebrush still
medicine beneath them.

A List of Celebrities Who've Stayed at the El Rancho Hotel

1. Doris Day
The carpet grabbed her shoe. Her pearls snowflaked its deep red.

2. Humphrey Bogart
He sat under a framed elk head with a cigar.
A man sits with a cigar under Bogart's framed head.

3. Jane Fonda
She left her room in a scurry. A ghost sat down on her bed. It was all the words ever spoken, however, that dropped a finger on her cheek.

4. Katharine Hepburn
She never left her room. She was busy looking at the leaves
                              on the trees
                                 shimmer like apostrophes.

5. Ronald Reagan
The president shook hands with a photographer who shook hands with my uncle before my uncle was killed a few blocks up from the hotel.

6. Jean Harlow
She was stunned to see dark figures across the train tracks train tracks train tracks train tracks.

The Indian Capital of the World

man hit by train
man found dead possibly from exposure in a field
woman hit by semitruck attempting to cross freeway
woman found dead in arroyo
man hit walking across road
man found dead near train tracks
man found in tunnel
man found in arroyo
man was picked up by two other men then killed
man left in field with stab wound overnight
woman crushed to death by semi-truck while asleep in alleyway
woman dead from hit and run
man found murdered and dead in homeless camp
man found dead in a field
man found dead in a field
man found dead in a field
man found dead in a field
man found dead in a field
man found dead in a field
man found dead in a field
man found dead in a field
man found dead in a field
        dogs mauled his remains
              in the fields
                 in the fields in the fields
              in the fields
                field   fields
                   fields fields
            fields
              among flowers
               flowers
            among flowers   in the weeds

American Bar

this beer turns into another
        before a fist and a fist and another fist
to the face pale & blue

they held each other the night before
        before pushing away

boys only hold boys
        like bottles

such a terrible beauty to find ourselves beneath things
such a terrible beauty to witness men ripen

—

this town will kill you
steel talons thread raw wool into sidewalks

ruins shard stuck in asphalt shimmer
hazy red evening in smog heat

bulbs burst white & blue balloons
at the downtown carnival

fires set in alleys
there are a thousand ways to hear sirens

from the bottom of a pool

—

boys red hued stumbling beer first
      blue dark deep leather reek
dull white nail bed nail-bitten jawline
      listening to weeds at the bottom of the bottle

each one growing wings
      to become flower beetles
singing back to foghorns
      of coming trains

the ground lets itself whiten
      around blood frosted
where the body was
      where the mouth was left open

—

blue morning cloud
        the gray under
ice grows new face

here in the fields—
        a boy

pressed pink by the morning

        his name in the beating
of crows trying to fly

with mouthfuls of mosquitoes

Red Running Into Water

tsi'naajinii nishłį
pronounce the ł as water whistling through shadow
    on black bark
the į as boy wearing only yucca
      lake colored

tábąąhá báshíshchíín
the í is now mouth of narrow stream
      inside a pink mobile home with white skirting
the ą sounds like pulling hair
      from the throat
shaped like the á

táchii'nii dashícheii
the á now a head busted open
      red running into water
the í is the boy now naked
      red running into water

tódik'ǫzhí dashinálí
boy has the ó for mouth
      washed with memory of salt water
pronounce this á as rain cloud
    belly up
the í still the boy floating on the lake
      except it is a field
his mouth left ǫ

Love Letter to a Dead Body

on our backs in burr and sage
                             bottles jangle us awake
                 cirrhosis moon for eye

fists coughed up
                we set ourselves on fire

copy our cousins
                  did up in black smoke
          pillar dark in June

Drunktown rakes up the letters in their names
          lost to bone
                 horses graze where their remains are found

and you kiss me to shut me up
                my breath bruise dark in the deep

leaves replace themselves with meadowlarks
                     cockshut in larkspur

ghosts rattle bottle dark and white eyed
          horses still hungry
                there in the weeds

In the Fields

with lines from D. A. Powell

We unyoke owl pellets from marrow
in desert meadow. His mouth a pigeon eye,

a torch, a womb turned flower. He, still a boy
dug from cactus skull, undresses into bark

beetles. He unlearns how to hold a fist
with my hand. Bursts into dandelion

seeds. *We are all beautiful at least once.*
Mud water puddles along enamel.

Eyeteeth blossom into osprey. Our bones
dampen like snowmelt under squirrel grass.

We could be boys together finally
as milk vetch, tumbleweed, and sticker bush.

We can be beautiful again beneath
the sumac, yarrow, and bitter water.

Hózhǫ Nahásdlį́į́'
Hózhǫ Nahásdlį́į́'
Hózhǫ Nahásdlį́į́'
Hózhǫ Nahásdlį́į́'

Notes

"Naked" borrows lines from the poem "Tokinish" by James Thomas Stevens.

"The Indian Capital of the World" is a poem derived from various newspaper articles that focus on alcoholism and death in Gallup, New Mexico. Specifically, I feel it necessary to note "'Blood Money': Life and Death in Gallup, NM" by Nick Estes, published in *Indian Country Today*, and "Rash of Exposure Deaths in Gallup, N.M., Blamed on an Old Foe: Alcoholism" by Nigel Duara, published in the *Los Angeles Times*, which inspired the listing of deaths and images of dogs and remains.

The final "In the Fields" poem borrows lines from the poem "Boonies" by D. A. Powell.

Acknowledgments

Nistaago ahxéhee' nihidideeshnįįł.

I offer my gratitude to the following publications and their teams for publishing versions of these poems: *American Indian Culture and Research Journal, Apogee Journal, Blueshift Journal, Boston Review, Connotation Press: An Online Artifact, Hunger Mountain, James Franco Review, Ploughshares, RED INK, The Rumpus, Shade Journal, Spilled Milk Magazine, Waxwing, Word Riot,* and *Yellow Medicine Review.* Ahxéhee' for offering me space.

To my parents, Douglas and Durinda Skeets, ahxéhee'. You are the strongest people I know and all my successes are yours first.

To my siblings, RaeDawn, Mark, Mitchell, and Morgan, ahxéhee' for your continued support and humor. You all keep me humble.

To my entire extended family, especially my cousins and aunts, ahxéhee'. You represent amazing courage. I want to especially offer my gratitude to my cousins Brendan James, the late Julian Skeet, Irwin Dawes, Stormy Dawes, and Anthony Skeet Jr. Ahxéhee' for showing me the many ways to survive. This book is dedicated to the late Benson James.

To my mentors Sherwin Bitsui, Joan Naviyuk Kane, and Santee Frazier, ahxéhee'. This book would not exist without your words, light, prayers, critiques, and friendship. I have so much appreciation for the Institute of American Indian Arts low-residency MFA program and offer my thanks to the faculty, staff, and administration.

My work and intellect have been molded by the following writers, scholars, and organizers: shinalí Luci Tapahonso, Manny Loley, Laura Tohe, Orlando White, Natalie Scenters-Zapico, Rigoberto González, Natalie Diaz, Trevor

Dane Ketner, Ryan Dennison, tanner menard, Tori Cárdenas, Keioshiah Peter, Faith Baldwin, Amy Beeder, Dan Mueller, Jack Trujillo, Dr. Tiffany Lee, Dr. Jennifer Denetdale, Mary Bowannie, Dr. Lloyd Lee, Dr. Melissa Yazzie, Dr. Rachel Levitt, Dr. Adrianna Ramírez de Arellano, and Christopher Ramirez. Ahxéhee' for your teachings and support over the years.

To my undergraduate and MFA cohorts, ahxéhee' for your guidance and critiques. You made me a better poet, student, and human.

To the Love Shack Crew—Anna Eskeets, Craig Tom, Tamara Tsosie, Nikki Livingston, and Jordan Dickson—ahxéhee' for your friendship. I want to mention Jordan Dickson, who loaned me a hundred dollars once and asked me to dedicate my first book to him. So I also dedicate this book to Jordan Dickson. My thanks extend to the Tripod, Anastasia Harvey and Shantel Halkini. I treasure our days together. I also would like to thank Anderson Yazzie Jr., Crystal Littleben (Miss Navajo Nation 2017–2018), Brittany Tabor, Shawna Nelson, Shawna Sunrise, Monika Honeyestewa, Daniel Begay, Wyndsor Yazzie, and so many others for their friendship. Ahxéhee' nistaago.

To Joey, Mary, Chris, and everyone at Milkweed Editions, ahxéhee' for your vision, support, guiding light, and amazing voice.

To Beth Dial and the National Poetry Series, ahxéhee' for this amazing contest and honor. Also, to Ricardo Maldonado, Sophie Herron, and everyone at the 92Y Unterberg Poetry Center, ahxéhee' for the life-changing honor.

To Kathy Fagan, ahxéhee' for hearing my voice and offering it space.

To everyone at the Avedon Foundation, ahxéhee' for the use of my uncle's portrait as the cover for this book.

To Quanah Yazzie, ahxéhee' for your love and support. The world is waiting for your words.

The land, fireplace, medicine, and sunrise helped me write this book. I offer prayers and thanks for their guidance.

Finally, dear reader, ahxéhee' for spending time with these poems. I hope they offered some light and beauty.

Quanah Yazzie

JAKE SKEETS is Black Streak Wood, born for Water's Edge. He is Diné from Vanderwagen, New Mexico. Skeets holds an MFA in poetry from the Institute of American Indian Arts, and his work has been recognized as a winner of the 2018 Discovery/*Boston Review* Poetry Contest and has been nominated for a Pushcart Prize. He edits an online publication called *Cloudthroat* and organizes a poetry salon and reading series called Pollentongue, based in the Southwest. Skeets is a member of Saad Bee Hózhǫ: A Diné Writers' Collective and currently teaches at Diné College in Tsaile, Arizona.

milkweed
editions

Founded as a nonprofit organization in 1980, Milkweed Editions
is an independent publisher. Our mission is to identify, nurture and publish
transformative literature, and build an engaged community around it.

milkweed.org

Interior designed by Mary Austin Speaker
Typeset in Adobe Caslon and Huronia Navajo

Adobe Caslon Pro was created by Carol Twombly
for Adobe Systems in 1990. Her design was inspired by
the family of typefaces cut by the celebrated engraver
William Caslon I, whose family foundry served
England with clean, elegant type from the early
Enlightenment through the turn of the
twentieth century.

Huronia Navajo was designed by Ross Mills for
Tiro Typeworks in 2013. Its creation was part of
a broad effort to provide typographic support for
all American languages, and is one of a very small
number of fonts that support
Navajo diacriticals.